HOW TO FORMAT AN EBOOK

NO MISTAKES PUBLISHING, VOLUME II

GIACOMO GIAMMATTEO

INFERNO PUBLISHING COMPANY

"© 2017 Giacomo Giammatteo. All rights reserved. No part of this book may be reproduced or transmitted in any form or by any means, electronic or mechanical, including photocopying, recording or by any information storage and retrieval system, without written permission from the author, except for the inclusion of brief quotations in a review.

Inferno Publishing Company

Houston, TX

For more information about this book visit my website.

Edition ISBNs

Trade Paperback 978-1-940313-28-3

E-book 978-1-940313-27-6

Cover design by Natasha Brown

Book design by Giacomo Giammatteo

This edition was prepared by Giacomo Giammatteo gg@giacomog.com

ISBN: 978-1-940313-27-6

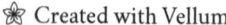 Created with Vellum

CONTENTS

1. How to Format an eBook — 1
2. Taking the First Steps — 5
3. The First Step — 9
4. Create Your First eBook — 13
5. Other Preferences — 23
6. A Chapter is a Chapter — 31
7. Heading Images — 35
8. Inline Images — 39
9. Preview — 47
10. Text Insertion — 57
11. Back Matter — 67
12. Editing — 73
13. Generate eBooks — 81
14. In Closing — 85

Acknowledgments — 91
Also by Giacomo Giammatteo — 93
About the Author — 97

HOW TO FORMAT AN EBOOK

*Y*ou've spent who knows how long writing your masterpiece. Don't ruin it all by giving your readers a bad experience with poorly formatted work.

But good formatters are difficult to find.

Tell me about it. My first book cost me $300 for formatting just the eBook. The work was done well, but it took forever (or seemed like it) and the company was inflexible on timing. It took more than three weeks to format the book and, let me tell you, those three weeks seemed like three years. The company also charged heavily to fix mistakes.

Later, I found another formatter who did the work much less expensively (and faster), but I ended up with other problems. And most of the time, the problems weren't his fault.

Sometimes timing was an issue. Because he was good and inexpensive, he was busy, so he often wouldn't have the time to format a manuscript when I was ready. And, as you all know, after spending so much time getting that far (to the formatting stage), you want it done *right then*.

I would also forget things—like the ISBN or the cover image or the acknowledgments. When this happened, I would have to send the missing materials to him, and wait for him to add that material to the book. Even though it didn't cost me nearly as much money as before, the waiting time killed me. Sometimes, the guy didn't even charge me for the service, but I still had to wait.

Then I found Vellum.

What is Vellum?

Vellum is the reason I'm writing this book. Because once I got accustomed to using it, there was no going back. Vellum makes it so easy to professionally format your book that I'm amazed it has taken somebody as long as it did to come up with such an app. Don't get me wrong, there have been many contenders for *the* app, but Vellum takes the cake.

With regard to cost, it's a bargain. And timewise, it's more of a bargain. I can format a book (start to finish) in one night, after dinner, and still have time to watch a show on TV—if I can find one worth watching. If I can't, I can format a second book. When I'm finished, I'll have files for Kindle, Apple, Nook, Google, and Kobo. I'll have saved almost a hundred bucks, and most importantly, I'll have saved a minimum of a week of waiting.

An author friend of mine first told me about Vellum. I was skeptical at first. I'd tried other so-called "easy-to-use" apps, but they were not so easy to use.

Nonetheless, I was growing frustrated with waiting on eBook production, so I gave it a try.

Cost

Let's get this part out of the way first. Vellum has several options for purchase.

- The cost for producing one book is $29.

- The cost for ten is $99
- The cost for unlimited books is $199

The $199 seems like a lot—until you do the math. Let's look at it.

Let's assume for a minute that formatting an eBook costs about $100. Some of you may get it done for less and some more, but $100 is a reasonable amount for a professionally formatted book.

Based on that number, the cost for doing one book would save you about $70.

Ten books would cost you $9.99 each (based on the $99 plan), so if you did all ten using Vellum, it would save you $900.

From that point on, the savings only get greater. I've got about sixteen books now. If I had used Vellum for all of them (based on $100 per book for normal formatting) and using the "unlimited" program for accounting, I would have saved about $1,400 (plus $100 on every book in the future).

But that's not the real benefit. The real advantage to using Vellum is the time you'll save. As I said, I can produce a book in one night, after dinner, and upload it to all of the big retailers without breaking a sweat; in fact, just before I started writing this, I did just that and also uploaded the book to StreetLib, PublishDrive, and Xin Xii. As a matter of fact, PublishDrive rejected a few of my earlier books, so I reformatted them using Vellum and they were approved on the first pass.

And if that weren't enough, when you use Vellum properly, the quality is second to none. Vellum lets you do things like drop caps, indentations, ornamental scene breaks, chapter headings with images etc., and all with no fuss. It's as easy as setting a preference (which is what it is), and they give you a variety of styles to select from.

But for me that's still not the best part of using Vellum. (I'm beginning to sound like a late-night TV program, aren't I?) The best part is the ease of editing.

When self-publishing, you invariably forget something like an acknowledgment or a link, or a reader spots a typo—or worse, an error, and points it out to you. This is something you *should* want to fix. In pre-Vellum days, I had to contact the formatter, apprise him of the error, wait for him to have time to fix it, then pay for the fixing. Now, all I have to do is open Vellum, fix the problem, and regenerate the files. Depending on the complexity of the error, it usually takes just a few minutes (less than ten).

So now that I've told you what Vellum can do, let's take a moment to look at how easy it is.

TAKING THE FIRST STEPS

The title of this chapter is "Taking the First Steps" but the first steps are not physical steps. You don't have to even move.

Like most things in life, learning to use a new app is a little challenging and, of course, may appear daunting. Few people like change, and learning to use a new app constitutes change.

Here is where Vellum shines. They have mastered the art of reducing learning to an "easy-as-pie" process. I'm not a computer or technology guru, and I learned to use Vellum in one day, formatting my first book within four to five hours. And it came out great.

Below is the cover file it generated from the image I provided. It gave me books for all five of the big retailers, and allowed me to produce a generic ePub file in case I wanted to use a distributor like Smashwords.

Below the cover image are screenshots of what the final product looked like on the copyright page, table of contents (which was automatically generated), dedication, introduction, and first chapter. I included these to let you see how Vellum handled each of the parts of the book and how Vellum generated the drop caps I chose.

cover image for novella

Table of Contents

screenshot for table of contents

Copyright Page

Inferno Publishing Company

ISBN: 978-1-940313-17-7

❦ Created with **Vellum**

For more information about this book, visit,
http://giacomogiammatteo.com

ISBN: 978-1-940313-17-7 (ebook)

Copyright © 2016 by Giacomo Giammatteo

All rights reserved.

No part of this book may be reproduced in any form or by any electronic or mechanical means, including information storage and retrieval systems, without written permission from the author, except for the use of brief quotations in a book review.

sample copyright page

D edication and Introduction

INTRODUCTION

I dedicated this book to Clayci. She has been a tremendous help on my road to recovery.

Our mother said that sisters should never be separated. That sisters were like twins that weren't born on the same day. When I was little I believed that—that, and a lot more.

She said that she'd never let us be hurt. That no

dedication and introduction

First Chapter

(With ornamental chapter heading and drop caps)

GRADUATION DAY

*T*hey say rookie cops have the best chance of getting killed the first year on the job. They say rookie cops are afraid to take a hit. They say rookie cops make all the mistakes. I heard all the talk, but no matter what they say, I say bullshit. No way this rookie cop was letting any of

sample first chapter

I don't know about you, but I love the drop caps, and I think the chapter headings and ornamental scene breaks look great too. I use different images on my mystery books, but they're easy to manage with Vellum.

By the way, when you are editing, ignore the triangle you see in the top-right corner of the image menu. It's a warning that the image is too small, but that little triangle will not show up in the final book.

But now I'm getting ahead of myself, and I swore I wouldn't do that. So let's go back to the beginning and take it one baby step at a time. If you discover that you're a faster learner or that you already are familiar with any of the processes, feel free to skip that information. You can always jump back to that chapter.

One more thing to note. While reading, if you discover that the image is too small to be read easily, simply click on it and it will open up larger.

THE FIRST STEP

To do this right, let's take a few baby steps. No, I don't mean literally walking like a baby, I mean in your head. After all, that is the biggest obstacle to anything. Before you do something, you have to make up your mind to do it (as I mentioned in the last chapter). Commit yourself. That's why people, in general, resist change. They don't want to commit to changing.

So now that you've committed to learning something new (you have, haven't you?), go buy Vellum. Get ready, then click on the link and pull out your credit card.

But first, you have to decide which package you want. If you're only going to format one book, get the $29 option. If you're planning on formatting more than three but less than fourteen, go for the $99 option for the first ten, and then if needed, you can purchase more at the individual price. If you plan on formatting more than fourteen books, go for the unlimited option, which is $199.

For most people the $99 option is the best deal, but for those of you who plan on writing (or formatting) a lot of books the unlimited deal is better. (And as you'll see later, you can use it for a lot more than books.)

The Next Step

Now that you've bought (and downloaded) Vellum, it's time to create your book.

Get everything ready. By everything, I mean any and all materials you will need to make your book. That includes…

…your .docx file.

Vellum requires a .docx file for import. If you write using Scrivener (and you should), export your manuscript using the compiler and select .docx as the format. It produces a clean file that will be ready to import. (Make sure to adjust your compile settings the way you want the manuscript to appear.) If you're not up-to-speed on using Scrivener, go to Gwen Hernandez's site and read her blogs. She also has a book—*Scrivener For Dummies,* which is fantastic.

If you don't use Scrivener, you can create a .docx file with the most recent versions of Word or Pages.

You will also need a properly sized cover image. Here are some rules from Vellum's website:

- Recommended Size
- Feedback from Vellum
- Marketing Image

Publishing an eBook requires that it have a cover image. When you assign a cover image, Vellum checks that it meets each store's requirements. When generating eBooks, Vellum creates a marketing cover image for each store, which you can upload along with your eBook.

Recommended Size

If you want to publish to every store supported by Vellum, you should start with a cover image that meets the largest size requirement. The specific dimensions depend on the *aspect ratio* of the cover or the relationship between its width and height. Visit Vellum's website (listed above) and read the section on cover images.

Below is an example of what one of my books looks like.

cover image of Writing Shortcuts book

Besides a cover image, you'll need any other images that you plan to use for chapter headings, scene breaks, or inline images. You'll also need all of your front and back matter, such as: ISBNs; copyright page info; Acknowledgments; your author bio; a list of other books you've written; and links (not store links) to social media, websites, and other related sites. Include a sample chapter if you plan on using one, and don't forget a review request, which should always be included.

I'm sure I've forgotten a few things, but it doesn't matter. You should know what you want in your book. So get *everything* prepared and in a logical place. But don't worry, if you forget something it's easy to fix.

GIACOMO GIAMMATTEO

Now that you have it all together, you're ready to...

CREATE YOUR FIRST EBOOK

You've purchased Vellum and your files are ready. It's time to create your book. It's easy. Open Vellum, then create a new file. Go to "My Book/Book Info." You should have a screen that looks like the following:

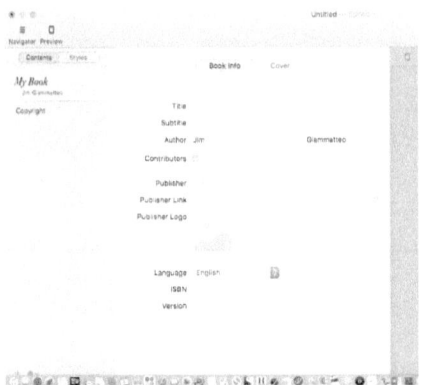

menu for adding cover image, publisher information, etc.

Insert your title and your subtitle if appropriate. Your author name should be filled out from information you supplied when you purchased Vellum. If it's wrong, simply change it.

Add any contributors that you want to list, such as editor or cover artist. If you don't want to add any, leave that blank.

Put the publisher information: name, website, and logo in the appropriate place.

List which language the book is in, the ISBN, and which version of the book it is, if appropriate.

Next, click on the tab for cover and insert the cover image, paying attention to the requirements.

At the bottom of the page, it asks for the ISBN and edition number. These fields only accept numbers, not letters. So the ISBN should be a 13-digit number and the edition should reflect which edition it is using numbers—1, 2, and so on.

If you try to enter a letter or symbol, it will cause the file to freeze. If you make a mistake and it does freeze, simply save your progress, quit Vellum, then restart it and everything should be fine.

Preferences

There aren't many preferences to fool with for Vellum, which is nice.

You have the Text Editor, where you can select from a small offering of fonts and sizes. That should be easy enough. If you have doubts, try them out and see what you like.

The next thing to look at in preferences is the section dealing with Store Links. This outstanding feature is crucial.

Rather than me trying to explain how the Store Links feature works, I thought I'd let Vellum's wonderful customer support tell you how it works. I'll explain it briefly, but the website (linked to below) offers a more detailed explanation.

The quickest explanation is that Store Links allow you to link to individual stores and/or sites where your book is sold, and to do so without offending or breaking the "rules" set by the retailers. So if a person is reading your book with a Kindle app, the links will take that person to Amazon. If they are reading an iBook with their iPhone or iPad, it will take them to Apple. It will do the same for Barnes and Noble, Kobo, and Google.

Store Links

With Store Links, you can take your reader to an online store to find more of your books, like the next book in a series, or other works in your catalog.

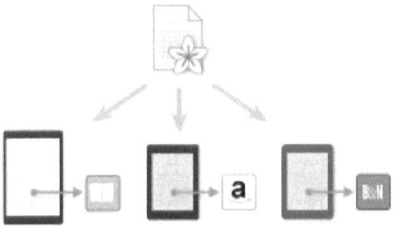

screenshot of how store links works (from Vellum's website)

Store Links take a reader to the store where they bought your book—your Kindle eBook links to Amazon, while your ePub version links to the Apple (or B&N, Kobo, or Google) Store. That means readers are able to buy at their preferred stores, and that your book will be safe from the rejection that can happen when linking to the wrong store.

Affiliate Codes

Affiliate programs allow you to earn revenue if a reader purchases products within a short amount of time after clicking on your store links. If you are a member, you can specify your affiliate codes in this section.

You can learn more about each store's affiliate program by going to the site associated with each store.

- Amazon
- iTunes

- [Barnes & Noble](#)
- [Kobo](#)

I might add that Store Links is also fantastic for using in the back matter for reviews. I always have a line at the end of the book that looks like this:

And don't forget to leave a review!

Looks simple enough, right? But it is deceiving because of Vellum's magnificent Store Links capabilities. When a person clicks on the "review" link, it will take them to the platform of their choice. So if they're using a Kindle to read, it will whisk them to Amazon (the link you provided when you filled out the Store Links.). If you're using a Nook device, it will take you there. If you're using an iPad or iPhone, it will take you to the site you designated for Apple, and so forth. It's fantastic. (Please note that if you use a generic ePub, which you might have to if you're going through a distributor, then the eBook store links will be sent to the "generic" link you provided.)

For any book sales, I have people steered to a page on my website (either the mystery site or the publishing site), which then has links to all of the larger retailer sites so a reader can buy where they want. Click this link to see. It goes to my No Mistakes Publishing site.

The Next Step

Now you're ready to take the next step. Go to the "Chapter Menu/Convert to Menu," then select "Copyright." Once you've done that, put in what you want. (You can view another ebook to see how it's done if you don't know.) Or, you can look at the copyright page in this book and fashion yours after that if you like. Keep in mind, however, that the page in this book is the page I use for nonfiction books. The fiction books have an additional disclaimer mentioning that it is a work of fiction.

Then go to the "File" menu and select "Reimport" to find your .docx file. All other files will be grayed out, so if you did your job right in the preparation stage, the .docx file should be easy to locate.

Vellum imports the files quickly, and it separates them into chapters based on your file. If it makes any mistakes, simply scan the "Navigator" section (on the left), look for any chapters labeled "untitled" and fix them. A fix usually involves simply converting to a "Chapter" using the aforementioned menu, then renaming it to the chapter title.

Here is what it might look like with errors. This screenshot (next page) shows a different type of error. Because the file I imported wasn't formatted properly, the chapter names didn't translate right. As you see, it only shows the chapter number, not title. It's easy to fix, though. Just go to the chapter name and type it in or use copy and paste. That's it. It's done. On the next pages are images of the error and then what it should have looked like.

My Book
Jim Giammatteo

Chapter 1
Chapter 2
3. Hard Times
Chapter 4
Chapter 5
Chapter 6
Chapter 7
Chapter 8
Chapter 9
Chapter 10
Chapter 11
Chapter 12
Chapter 13
Chapter 14
Chapter 15
Chapter 16
Chapter 17
Chapter 18
Chapter 19
Chapter 20
Chapter 21
Chapter 22
Chapter 23

screenshot of a error-filled import

How to Format an eBook
Giacomo Giammatteo

Copyright
1. How to Format an eBook
2. Taking the First Steps
3. The First Step
4. Create Your First eBook
5. Other Preferences
6. A Chapter is a Chapter
7. Heading Images
8. Inline Images
9. Preview
10. Text Insertion
11. Back Matter
12. Editing
13. Generate eBooks
14. In Closing
Acknowledgments
Also by Giacomo Giammatteo
About the Author

what the chapters should look like when viewed in the Navigator

Spacing

Many books will have spacing issues. This isn't a problem exclusive to Vellum; it's an issue with almost all formatting. Luckily, it's a quick and easy fix too.

If you look at the right-hand preview side of Vellum, you'll see how the content appears after importing with improper spacing. Some people might like this. I don't. This screenshot is followed by another one after I adjusted the spacing.

spacing issues

Screenshot before adjustment (above) and after adjustment (below).

after spacing is adjusted

Adjusting the Spacing

Adjusting the spacing was simple. It could have been fixed in Scrivener or even in Word prior to importing, but if you imported it with problems, it's easy to fix.

Click on the "Styles" button on the upper-left-hand side. Now, click on "Body" at the bottom left. Your screen should look similar to this:

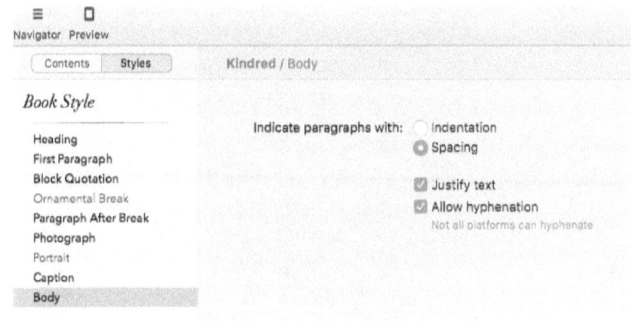

menu for styles

Make sure that the button for "Spacing" is checked under the "Indent Paragraph With" feature on the right-hand side, and voilà! Your spacing problems are fixed, and your work looks much more professional.

If you happen to have any extra carriage returns in your work, delete them. You could have accomplished this by inserting carriage returns but that inserts too much space between paragraphs, and it signals Vellum to begin a scene break, which is not something you want to do.

I'm not going to go through Vellum's excellent technical support/customer service features, but when it comes to dealing with chapters, whether it's making a new one, splitting an existing one into multiple chapters, or merging several chapters together, Vellum has it covered. And it's easy to do.

Other Fixes

Assuming you have other fixes you want to make, simply make them. In Vellum, it's easy.

Now that you've mastered that part, let's move on to...

OTHER PREFERENCES

As we've already seen, the preferences menu is sparse. But that doesn't mean that is all you have to decide. Vellum lets you control how your book will look, and it does it by allowing you to *see* the differences.

Look at the top of the "Navigator" (the panel on the left-hand side) and click on the "Styles" tab. Your screen should look like the screenshot below (or the next page, depending on which device you're using).

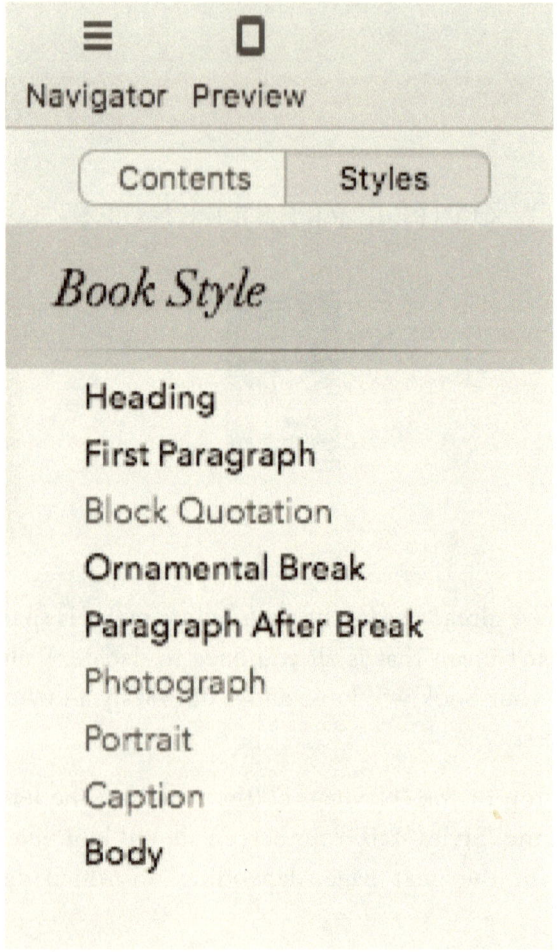

styles menu

As you can see it provides you with choices of how you want your book to appear, down to the tiniest detail: Heading, First Paragraph, Block Quotation, Ornamental Break, Paragraph After Break, Photograph, Portrait, Caption, and Body. When you combine these things, it gives you complete control over the outcome of your masterpiece.

HOW TO FORMAT AN EBOOK

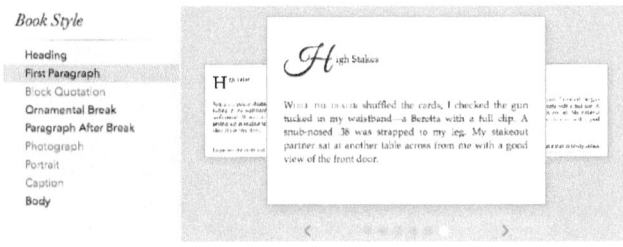

options for styles

The screenshot above shows a sample of what the "Kindred" option looks like for the first paragraph. If you click on the arrows shown at the bottom of the screenshot, it will display a different sample. You simply select the one you like and move on to the next preference in styles.

The next choice deals with block quotations and Vellum has some interesting options. I happen to like the one shown below, but there are plenty to choose from.

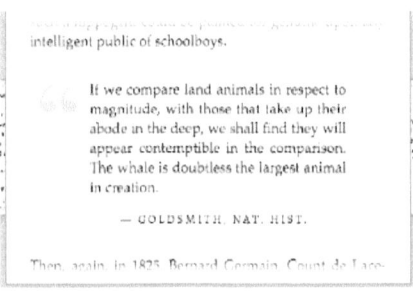

block quotation options

After block quotations, we move to the setting dealing with paragraph after a scene break. I feel this is an important one, so you should take time to really analyze it.

W hile the dealer shuffled the cards, I checked the gun tucked in my waistband—a Beretta with a full clip. A snub-nosed .38 was strapped to my leg. My stakeout partner sat at another table across from me with a good view of the front door.

I squeezed the cards and stared at a pair of lovely ladies. Not a bad hand to start with, especially when the guy to my right, a notorious bluffer, just

scene break options

The next option is for "Photographs." I realize that not everyone will have photographs in their book, but if you do, it's nice to have this option. This is an option showing a "grayed" shadow surrounding the picture. They have options with white, with no shadow, etc. Plenty to choose from. As a side note, due to the ease of using Vellum, combined with Pronoun's (a distributor) new policies regarding download fees from Amazon, I have begun inserting images into all my books, even the mysteries. People seem to love it.

image options

The next choice is another one that not many people will need, but for those who do it's an outstanding option. That is, "Portrait" and it's followed by the option for the type of caption an author may want.

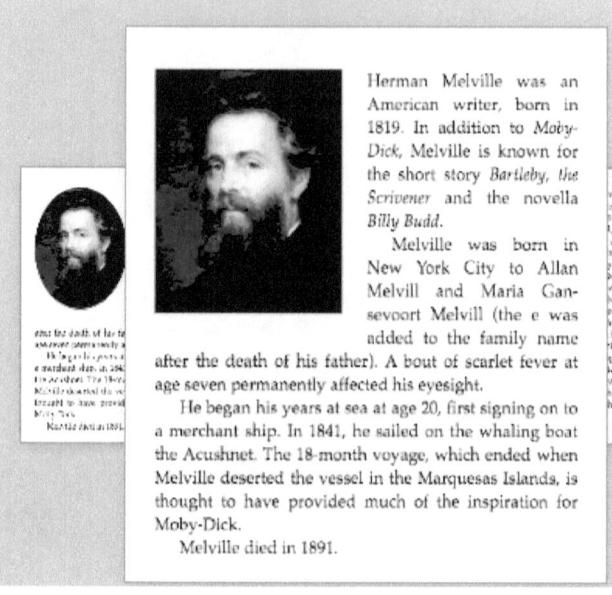

photograph images and alignment

caption choices

We'll end up with a few choices on body text. How do you want to show paragraphs—with spacing or indentation? Do you want the text justified? And do you want to allow hyphenation?

Indicate paragraphs with: ● Indentation
                            ○ Spacing

☑ Justify text
☑ Allow hyphenation
   Not all platforms can hyphenate

paragraph choices

As I said, the control Vellum gives you is amazing, so take advantage of it and make the book yours.

A CHAPTER IS A CHAPTER

A chapter is a chapter, right?

Not necessarily so. Some writers, myself included, write using different points of view. Using different chapter headings, especially combined with images, is a fantastic way of letting the readers know which character's point of view (POV) is being shown.

It's probably easier if I show you. The following screenshots are from my eBook *Murder Takes Patience* one of the mysteries in my Friendship & Honor series. The screenshots may appear on the next page, depending on which device you're using.

CHAPTER 1

A Strange Goodbye

heading image

The badge image indicates it's from the detective's POV, and the gun image (below) indicates it's from the hit man's POV.

Even if the reader isn't paying close attention, it's difficult to mess that up. For some of my other series I use handcuffs or a bullet. Either way, once you have established what you're doing, the rest is easy.

CHAPTER 4

A Special Favor

heading image

The best thing is that Vellum makes it easy. Simply go to the "Navigator" (remember, the left-hand window), select the chapters that you want (in this case, I would select all first-person POV chapters one time and all third-person the next), then go to the "Chapter Menu" and select Heading, "Add Heading Image." It will insert a heading image in all chapters you select.

Assigning Heading Images to Multiple Elements

To assign the same heading image to multiple elements, select the elements you want to affect in the Navigator, and then use the **Heading** section of the **Chapter** menu:

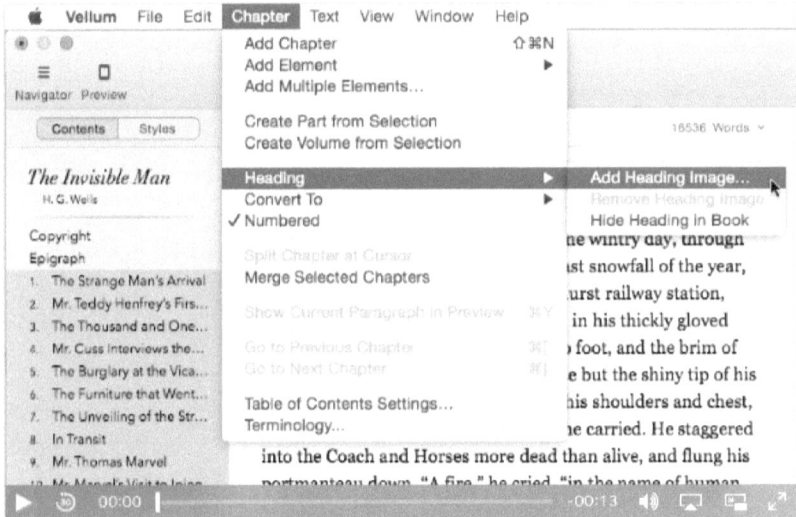

How to use heading images

This might seem like a chore, but it isn't so bad. The way I do it is to select *all* of the chapters, use the Add Heading Image so that it inserts an image in all of them (like the badge for first-person POV), then go back and select only third-person POV chapters and use Add Heading Image again to insert the gun image. Doing it this way, I can insert chapter headings in the entire book with just a few steps.

That's it. You're done. And not only do you have an eBook that looks fantastic, it's one people will remember.

Verify

When you're done, verify that you've done it right; in fact, you should do this with everything. Use the *preview* option to see how your book will appear on a variety of devices. Remember, not everyone reads on an iPad. In many third-world countries, phones are the preferred choice for reading.

But let's take a look at heading images before we get to Preview.

HEADING IMAGES

Here's a link to Vellum's help on their website. It should have up-to-date information for future use.

*C*hoose "Add Heading Image" to embellish a chapter heading with an illustration, photograph, or other picture.

At the beginning of this chapter, I used "Add Heading Image" to insert the image of a screenshot I had taken of Vellum, displaying the "Navigator," "Text Editor" and "Preview." For all of the other chapters, I used an image of the cover of this book. The entire process didn't take more than a few minutes. Prior to using Vellum, it would have taken me hours.

I use images for most of my mystery novels to indicate POV (as mentioned in the last chapter). It's a simple process, and if I want to apply it to multiple chapters, I simply select them in the left-hand pane (Navigator), then go the "Chapter Menu" and hit, "Heading/Add Heading Image." It's as easy as that.

I recently decided to add heading images to all chapters in one of my grammar books, so I selected all chapters in the left-hand pane (Navigator), then inserted the *dictionary* image you see below. In an instant, I was rewarded with a heading image inserted into *all* chapters, and it was done perfectly.

WORDS DIFFICULT TO PRONOUNCE

There are some words that are difficult to pronounce. I'm not talking about the regional pronunciations you find, like the penchant for saying "wooder" instead of "water," which is common in the Baltimore to Philly area, or the differences between crayfish and crawfish. I'm not talking about that. I'm speaking of the mispronunciations of common (often imported) words.

Which words am I speaking of? Let's look at a few from the list below. I've included links for each entry so you can hear how to pronounce them correctly:

another example of heading image

There is not much that could be easier than that. It beats the hell out of learning complicated html code, or learning how to use other complicated apps that allow you to do this.

Vellum is so easy that it has gotten to where I create ePubs for almost everything. I've already mentioned the checklists, but my wife uses it to send and share her recipes also. And my sister (who she shares them with) loves it. It makes it easy to read, she knows where it is. (She stores them on her iPad.) and she has almost continuous access to her iPad and, therefore the recipes.

In fact, my sister liked it so much that she decided to make a family recipe book to give out as Christmas gift. At first, she was going to use a well-known service, but they wanted about fifty dollars apiece. I told her we could do it ourselves, then have it printed for about twenty percent of the cost. Even considering the cost of a book cover, she saved money, as she intended to give out quite a few books.

All of that would be enough to convince me, but we're not done yet. Look below to see a sample. The image you see is going to be the one used for the recipe for Mama's famous lasagna.

inline image example

PS. I couldn't put the actual recipe in or my wife would have killed me.

INLINE IMAGES

Some of this chapter is taken from Vellum's website help section because they explain it far better than I could. And here's a link to use, as Vellum is pro-active and continually updates their information. I wouldn't want you to be behind or out-of-date regarding your information.

Inline Images

Inline Images can be used for anything. Most books don't include a large number of images due to the cost of formatting them. (That's now changed for me.) There is also the added cost Amazon tacks on for file size. I think they charge about fifteen cents per megabyte. In comparison, Apple lets you use up to two gigabytes. I did a blog post on this comparing the various services. It's almost criminal how much Amazon charges. (There is a way around this using Pronoun. See my *eBook Distribution* book to learn how.)

Anyway, back to the subject at hand. There are some types of books that demand pictures, like cookbooks, children's books, art books, or certain history books and other nonfiction books that contain charts or tables. If you're writing one of them, make sure you are aware of the book size.

One nice feature that Vellum offers is the ability to adjust the size of the image right on the screen, and it's all done with the click of a button. Below is an image I inserted for an example.

picture of meatballs cooking as inline image

When you click on the triangle in the upper-right corner, you should see the image below.

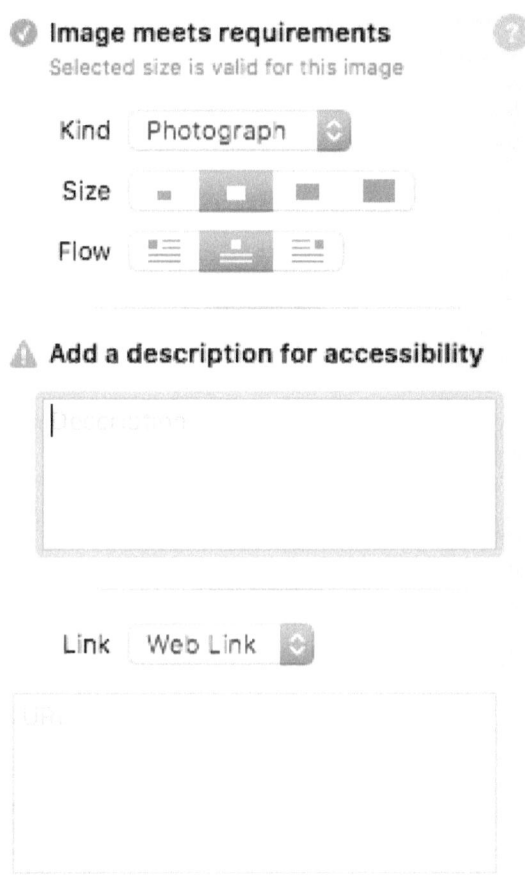

inline image adjustments

The first thing you'll notice is a green check saying that the image meets the requirements. If you're not greeted by that green check, then something is wrong, and it's usually the size of the image you are attempting to use.

After that, you'll see a drop down menu for what kind of image it is. This makes a difference in how the image is displayed. The choices are: Photograph, Figure, Portrait, Freestanding, or Bookcover. You can see how your choice affects the display in the Preview pane or by reading about it in Vellum's excellent help section.

If it's the image size, adjust that. Once you get the green check, look below it and you'll see the size options. You can go small, medium, large, or full size. You'll be able to see how the changes will affect the work, as they will be reflected in the Preview pane, and you can adjust the Preview to display what it would look like on various devices.

Below the size options are options for alignment—left, center, or right alignment. Choose which one you want. And below that is a spot to enter in a description of the image. At the bottom, you can add a link. This can be a web link or a store link.

Adding an Image

As with adding heading images, adding photo images to your book is a cinch with Vellum. Simply place the cursor where you want the image to appear, go to the "Add Text Feature" menu, and then choose "Add Image." (I think it's the third one down.) It will then take you to a window that looks similar to the one below, where you can navigate to the image you want, or do a search for the image, then select it.

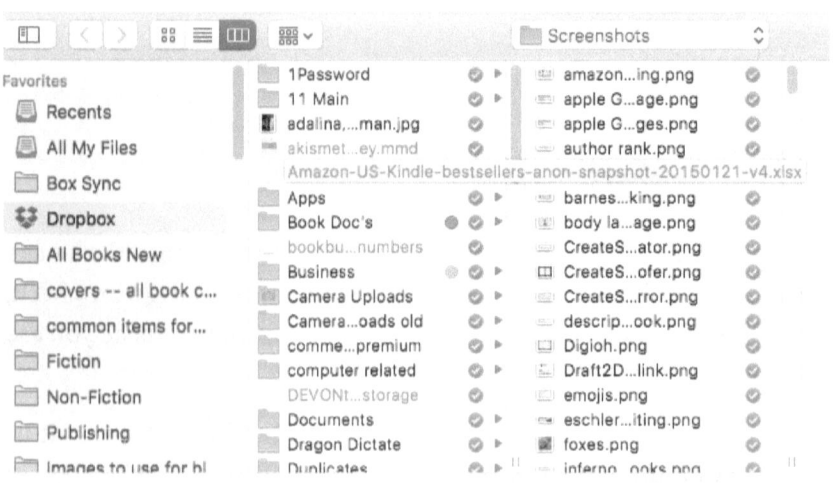

This is a screenshot of the window I was presented with.

HOW TO FORMAT AN EBOOK

Screenshot of a portrait image done in two formats

The second image shows a picture displayed using different choices. Both are left-aligned (in the picture), but one uses Portrait and one Photograph as their option. The screenshot I used is obviously centered. You could change these options by selecting left, center, or right alignment, and also by choosing how you want the captions displayed.

Screenshot of the menu for generating ebooks

The bottom image shows a screenshot of the menu for generating ebooks, and it shows what a file looks like when it's inserted using the Left-Align feature. This file has a book cover image. If the cover image were not included, the left side of the screenshot would be blank.

To make things simple, and to show you the flexibility of Vellum, I'll display a screenshot in all forms. Due to the space requirements, the images will probably display on two pages.

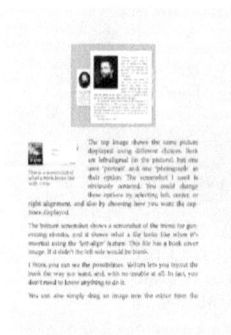

Screenshot when aligned left

Screenshot centered

I think you can see the possibilities. Vellum lets you layout the book the way *you* want and with no trouble at all; in fact, you don't need to know anything to do it.

You can also simply drag an image into the editor from the finder or your photo app or damn near anywhere. Once you drag it in, you can adjust it as I mentioned above.

One thing to note, the changes are not visible within the editor, but if you look to the right-

Screenshot aligned right

HOW TO FORMAT AN EBOOK

hand side at the Preview pane, you'll see how it will appear in an eBook. So, the screenshot below (the top one) shows how how all three images appear in the text editor, and the one below that shows how the same page appears in the Editor pane, and how it will appear in the book.

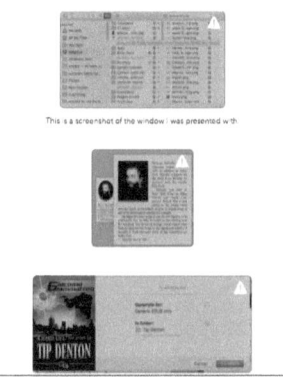

Text Editor

Shown in the Preview Pane

Notice the difference of the bottom picture. That's the one we changed the settings on. Also note that the first image is not shown, as that is displayed on the previous page.

For more details on how the settings affect your output, consult Vellum's help section.

One note: for displaying charts or graphics, use the Figure option.

If you are displaying book covers or images of other products, consider using the store links or regular links. Now lets take a look at the Preview pane.

PREVIEW

The Preview panel may be the most important function. Don't overlook it. "Preview" allows you to see what your book will look like on a variety of devices, like *iPhones*, *iPads*, Barnes and Noble's *Simple Touch*, Kobo's *Gio*, *Kindles*, and *Android* devices.

And it not only shows you how it will look on a variety of devices but in various fonts, sizes, and with other considerations, such as do you want to see how it looks when viewed originally, or in sepia, or when displayed in a night-viewing mode.

The first thing to do is access the device menu (shown below) and select the type of device you want to view it on. Assuming that you are distributing widely (which I hope you are) then you'll eventually want to view your book on all devices. Vellum allows these (for now):

iBooks

Apple iPad

Apple iPhone

Kindle

GIACOMO GIAMMATTEO

Fire

Paperwhite

Kobo

Gio

Nook

Simple Touch

Google Play

Android Tablet

iBooks
✓ iPad
iPhone

Kindle
Fire
Paperwhite

Kobo
Glo

Nook
Simple Touch

Google Play
Android Tablet

device selection menu

And this is what they look like on the various devices.

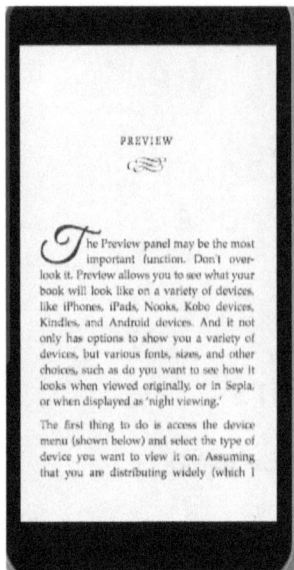

iPhone, set to Sepia

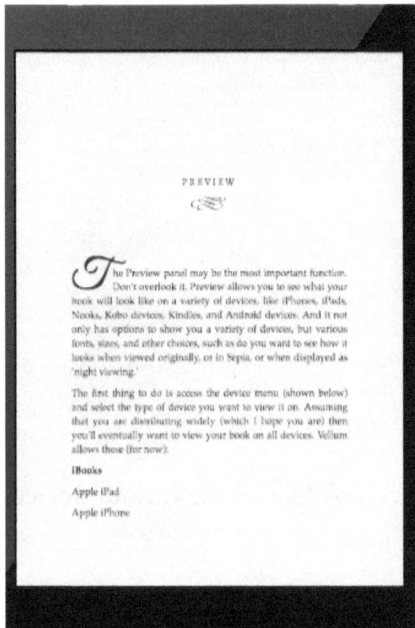

iPad, Sepia

HOW TO FORMAT AN EBOOK

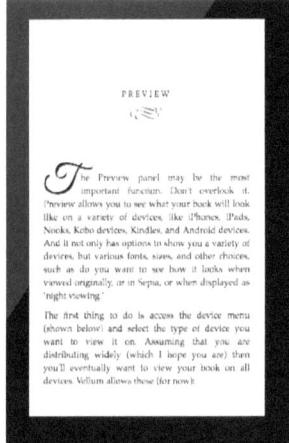

Kindle Fire, White

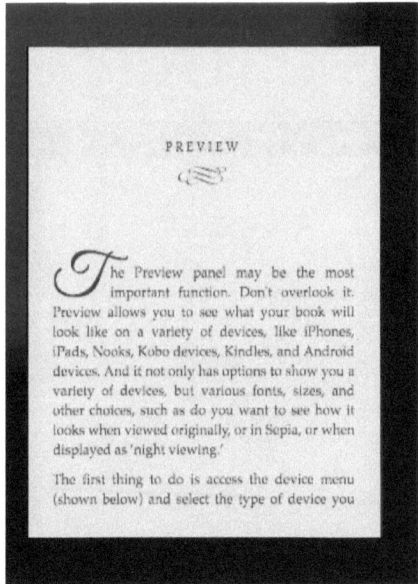

Kindle Paperwhite

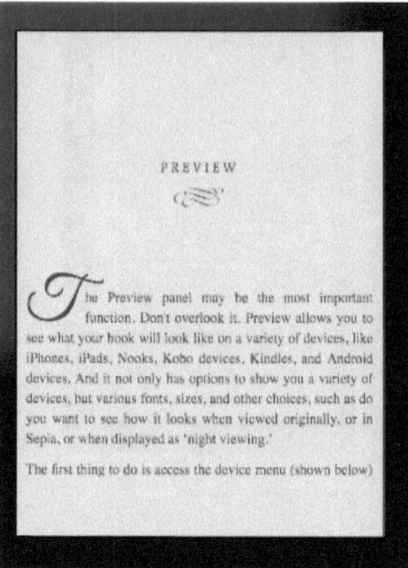

Kobo Gio

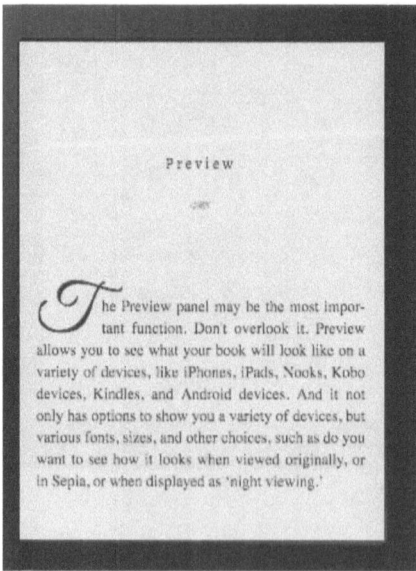

Nook Simple Touch

HOW TO FORMAT AN EBOOK

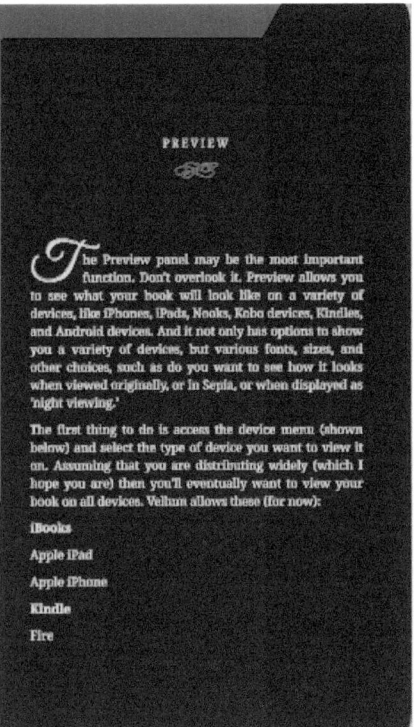

Google Play, Night

As if this weren't enough, you can use "Preview" to go through the book page by page, and see each correction you're making, and how a change will affect the final product.

For instance, this is the end of my author bio section. I decided to not only include crazy Dennis' picture, but links to some of my social media as well, and I wanted to see what it would look like. Here it is as it would appear on an iPhone.

author bio sample

You can use Preview to jump to any section of the book also. Simply access the menu near the top right of the "Preview" pane and it will drop down to this:

> 7. Capitalization
> 8. Words Difficult to Pronounce
> 9. More Mispronounced Words
> 10. Plurals of Compound Words
> 11. Misunderstood Idioms
> 12. He's Going Downhill
> 13. Eat, Shit, and Die
> 14. An Axe to Grind
> 15. Hunger Pangs
> 16. Shoo-in or Shoe-in
> 17. Thumbs-Up or Thumbs-Do...
> 18. Toe the Line
> 19. First Come, First Serve
> 20. How to Use Dates and Times
> 21. Wordiness
> 22. Very
> 23. Closing
> Also by Giacomo Giammatteo
> About the Author
> Acknowledgments

navigation menu on preview pane

By the way, at the top center of the "Preview" pane, it lists which device you are previewing, so there is no chance of getting mixed up.

Next to the drop-down table-of-contents menu, are two arrows for navigating to the previous chapter or the following one. Very handy. And at the top right of the "Preview" pane are two buttons, one for generating eBooks and one for showing them in the finder. There are menu options for both, but it's nice to have it easily accessible.

By the way, I think we mentioned this earlier, but when you are editing or doing general layout, forget what you see in the "Text Editor" and look at the "Preview" pane. That's what shows you how it will appear on various devices.

To be able to make changes and see, in real time, how it affects the appearance of the book is priceless. Vellum has done a magnificent job with this.

And not only does "Preview" show you how your book will appear, the "Preview" pane can also be used for verifying store links for each type of device. How? Easy.

Navigate to any store link you've created, then switch the preview to whichever device you want to test. If it's a Kindle Fire, it will whisk you to Amazon. If it's an iPad or iPhone you're testing, it will take you to the Apple store. In this way, you can verify your links work at each of the major distributors using their devices.

TEXT INSERTION

As I've already mentioned, I'm not trying to duplicate Vellum's outstanding technical support or tutorials (You can find the support pages here), but I would like to cover a few things that are important. One of them is the well-positioned and excellent option for text insertion.

This can be accessed under the text menu, but it's easier from the button at the top left of the main pane, the editor. Inside are many options, valuable options, including:

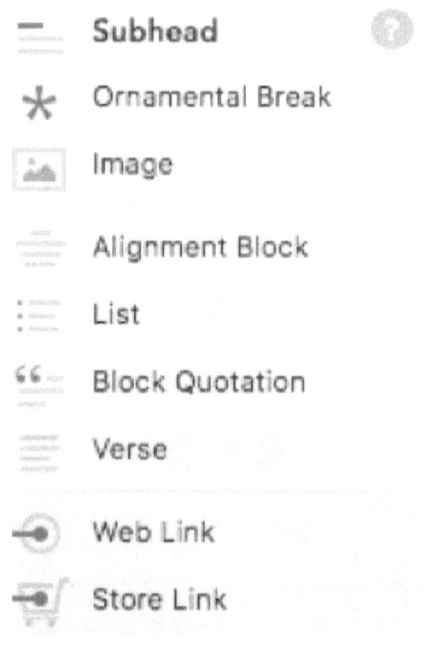

text insertion menu

Most of what you need to add/edit with will be found under the Add Text Feature menu. A rundown of the above-listed menu is necessary.

Subhead

THIS IS HOW A SUBHEADING LOOKS

If you have a section of a chapter that needs a subheading, this is where to do it. You simply highlight the text, then use the subheading feature. Vellum then inserts a subheading section (like above) so that you can type away. It's a good way of displaying your work when that is appropriate. It is especially useful for nonfiction books. I used it frequently in my No Mistakes Grammar books.

Don't forget what we talked about previously regarding how it appears in the Text Editor versus the Preview pane. When you convert something to a subheading in the Text Editor, it won't look significantly changed, but if you glance over to the Preview, you'll see it has been. The subhead will have been transformed into uppercase, and other formatting may have changed.

Ornamental Break

Vellum gives you a lot of choices for the type of Ornamental Break you want in the styles preferences, but no matter what you choose, it can have a significant impact if used properly.

In many books, adding an extra line or two signifies a lapse of time or some other form of scene break. An Ornamental Break is typically used for more dramatic shifts. Location shifts, major time shifts (as in more than hours), point of view changes (POV), etc.

I use both first- and third-person POV to tell my mysteries, so if I'm going to shift POV in the middle of the chapter, I need something more than an extra return. An Ornamental Break fits this bill perfectly.

Ornamental breaks can be lifesavers. Not only do they look great (depending on which one you choose) but they can serve your POV purposes, as I just mentioned.

When POV is restricted to a chapter, the heading image suffices and serves a fantastic purpose; however, if I need to switch POV in the middle of a chapter, the best way to indicate that (short of using another image) is with an ornamental break.

Image (inline image)

We've already talked about images. Just remember, if you need to use one, you can put it almost anywhere.

Alignment Block

An alignment block is just what it sounds like. If you need to change alignment on an image, a paragraph, or even a sentence, use this to do it.

This is a right-aligned piece of text.

This is center-aligned.

And this is the standard, left-aligned.

A lignment blocks are valuable for citing newspaper or magazine articles, dates, locations, etc.

One thing to note is that text within an alignment block, even left-aligned text, will not be formatted as the first paragraph of a chapter.

Center-aligned text is especially useful if you use text at the beginning of a chapter to indicate location—*where* the chapter is taking place—or *when* the chapter is taking place.

In my novel, *Murder Takes Time,* the story alternates between Brooklyn and the Philadelphia area, and it also switches in time. Because of that, I list where and when things are happening at the beginning of each chapter, as the following screenshot shows, where it says,

Brooklyn, New York--Current Day.

And note that it is centered and in italics. This serves to draw attention to it.

CHAPTER 1

RULE NUMBER ONE: MURDER TAKES TIME

Brooklyn, New York—Current Day

He sipped the last of a shitty cup of coffee and

alignment block sample

List

Lists are used for, well, exactly what you'd think they're used for. They're not always easy to display using other apps, but Vellum (once again) makes it a cinch. Simply highlight the text you want displayed as a list, go to the "Add Text Feature" menu and select "List." It comes out like this:

- Pick up the kids at 3:00
- Stop at the grocery store
- Jesse coming in at 7:30
- Don't forget to tape Blacklist

You could also choose to have it a numbered list instead of a bullet list. The default is a bullet list, but changing it is as simple as hitting the "Gear" menu to the right of the list and selecting "Numbered." It will produce a result like this:

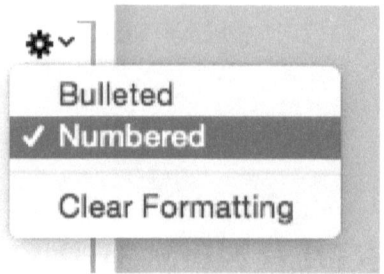

Screenshot showing Gear drop-down menu

1. Pick up the kids at 3:00
2. Stop at the grocery store
3. Jesse coming in at 7:30
4. Don't forget to tape Blacklist

You'll notice each item is automatically preceded by an incremental number. Below is an image of a numbered list I used for another book I'm writing on publishing.

1. Write a great book (See my other book, *No Mistakes Writing, Volume II*, for advice on how.)
2. Find a great editor.
3. Create a great cover.
4. Make sure the layout and formatting are superb.
5. Write an irresistible description and premise.
6. Proofread, proofread, proofread.
7. Price the book as if it's worth something.
8. Let the world know you're there.

numbered list sample

I frequently use bulleted and numbered lists in my nonfiction writing. They sure come in handy.

Block Quotation

Use the Block Quotation feature when you need to format a quotation because you want it to stand out (like maybe a dictionary definition) or because the quotation is too long for inclusion in a paragraph.

It's easy (I'm guessing you're getting used to hearing that phrase by now) to accomplish. Just highlight the text you want to cite and use the Add Text Feature menu to create the Block Quotation.

Block quotations also come in handy for—you guessed it—citing quotations. (I used them often in the No Mistakes Grammar series.) If you need a block quotation, not much else will suffice.

Below is an example of a block quotation. According to Brainyquote, Mark Twain said…

 Substitute "damn" every time you're inclined to write "very"; your editor will delete it and the writing will be just as it should be.

— MARK TWAIN

As you can see, the block quotation not only draws attention to the quote, it looks pretty damn good. Also note that I used the "Attribution" feature to add Twain's name, and it looks professional.

Attribution

Attributions are just that, attributions. So when you use the "Block Quotation" feature, a gear setting will appear to the upper-right portion of the block quotation once you click in it. Simply click on the gear and choose "Add Attribution."

The screenshot below shows what it will look like. I used the "Block

Quotation" feature to list "family is everything" and the gear to the right gives us the option of adding an attribution or clearing the formatting. The caption below the screenshot explains what the image is.

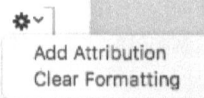

[Family is everything.

screenshot of Attribution option

Verse

For those of you who use verse, as in poetry, this is a priceless feature that will save you time and make your work look better and certainly more professional.

If you have verse you want to display, go to the "Add Text Feature" menu and select "Verse."

> *As you see, it will bring up a formatting block that centers the text and puts it in italics. This is perfect for lines of poetry, lyrics to a song (if you have the rights), and it can even be good for when you're citing text from a newspaper article.*
>
> — NOBODY

As with the block quotation feature, you can easily add an attribution.

Web Link

Some apps make inserting links into your work a chore; not Vellum. In fact, if you simply type a web address, like the one following this paragraph, Vellum automatically converts it to a link. Clicking on it allows you to edit it. nomistakespublishing.com

The following is from Vellum's website in their help section:

Note: to link to eBooks you should use the **Store Link** text feature (see below). And if you'd like to link to your Facebook or Twitter page, you can use an About the Author element, which also provides icons for those links.

BACK MATTER

We've already discussed the need for certain back matter. Now let's go into more detail.

First off. If you plan to use Vellum for more than one book, the following is invaluable:

Create a new Vellum file and make templates for all of your front and back matter. In mine, I have two copyright elements, one for fiction and one for nonfiction. I also have elements for Acknowledgements, Author bio, and Also by. I saved this file to my *books* folder and named it *Back and Front Matter*.

When it comes time to format a new book, I simply open the file, then drag and drop the elements from the *Back-and-Front-Matter file* to the new file, and I'm done.

Author Bio

In this day and age, people are curious about who you are and what you do. Give them something to chew on. It doesn't have to be much. No need for a full autobiography, but *something*, and something with a little substance. Here's what I include at the back of my books.

I start out with a pic of me and my favorite dog of all time, Slick.

Giacomo and Slick medium-sized image

Giacomo Giammatteo is the author of gritty crime dramas about murder, mystery, and family. He also writes nonfiction books including the No Mistakes Careers series, No Mistakes Grammar series, and the soon-to-be-released No Mistakes Publishing series.

When Giacomo isn't writing, he's helping his wife take care of the animals on their sanctuary. At last count they had 40 animals—7 dogs, a horse, 6 cats, and 26 pigs. Oh, and one crazy—and very large—wild boar, who takes walks with Giacomo every day and happens to also be his best buddy.

Giacomo and Slick small image

Side note: As you can see, using the option to resize the image and adjust the flow, I can easily change the way it appears. This took me all of three or four minutes to accomplish.

Then, I conclude with a picture of Dennis, our wild boar.

HOW TO FORMAT AN EBOOK

Dennis, the great and wonderful (He made me say that.)

This is enough for a bio. It tells people what I write, what I intend to write in the future, and it mentions what I do in my spare time. *And* it shows a picture of Dennis, which he insists upon.

Also By

If there is one thing that's imperative, this could be it. We're going to presume going in that readers will like your book. If they do, they will (hopefully) want to know what else you've written and where they can buy it. This is *exactly* what you want. You don't want them putting the book down and forgetting about you; you want them to buy another book right then. So don't make it difficult. Include links that will take them to where the books are sold. See the part on Vellum's Store Links for more on this.

Acknowledgments

This is another section that you don't want to forget or ignore. This is the perfect place to publicly thank your beta readers for all the hard work they've done. And let's face it, even if you don't sell many books, beta readers like to see their name in print. It will make them work harder for you the next time, and you definitely want them working harder. It's difficult to find inconsistencies in one's own work; the more beta readers you have and the more loyal they are, the better your chances of writing a better book.

If you're stuck on what to say, pick up almost any book and look. I'm sure there will be an acknowledgments section.

Mailing List

If you can't forget the "also by" part, you also can't forget to include a link to your mailing list. Having a decent mailing list to send notices to is imperative. You need to let them know what you're doing, and you especially need to let them know when you're coming out with a new book.

I know of several authors who have way more than ten thousand people on their mailing list. I don't have near that many, but I haven't put the proper amount of time into it. Some of the more-established big-name authors have more than one hundred thousand. Mailing lists can be crucial to sales. Don't ignore them. The good thing is that the people who tend to sign up for mailing lists are the same ones who tend to buy.

Review Request

If a mailing list is imperative, a review request is pretty damn important. If you've been in the business for any amount of time, you know how tough it is to get an honest review, and like it or not, reviews do drive sales.

I'm not saying that they determine if a book will be successful or not, but they do help. If a book has hundreds of good reviews and few negative ones, it is bound to earn a few more sales. And, the people who review it after just reading it will lean toward a favorable review (assuming you wrote a good book).

So don't leave this hanging. Ask for a review and tell them how to do it.

Sample Chapter

Some authors are big on this. Others are not. If you are the kind of author who favors this, make sure to include a sample chapter of your next book and tell the reader when to expect it.

It's my opinion that you shouldn't do this unless you plan on releasing the book within the next few months, but it's up to you.

The bottom line is that no matter what you decide to include, Vellum has an option for you and an easy way to make it happen.

The Convert To menu has the following options. With those options, you can easily convert anything to a chapter, acknowledgment, author bio, etc.

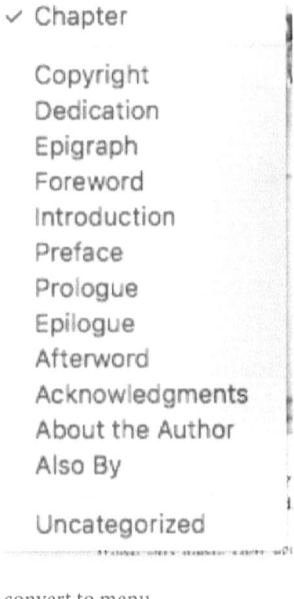

convert to menu

And, as we've already seen, the Text Insertion menu has additional options.

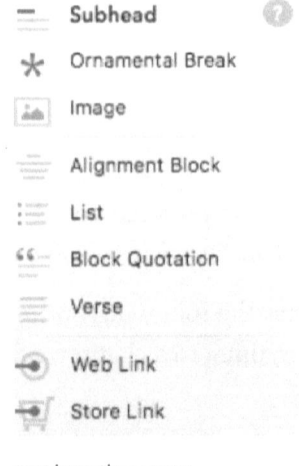

text insertion menu

By the way, for those of you who will be using Vellum often, here's an easy way to keep the back matter handy. (This is a repeat, but I felt it was worth mentioning again.)

1. Create a Vellum file.
2. Add an Acknowledgments, About the author, Also by, Copyright, and any other section you feel you'll need.
3. Fill out those with the information you use in your books.
4. Save the file as a separate Vellum file for easy access.

Now, whenever you need back matter for a book, simply open the aforementioned Vellum file side by side with your current WIP (work in process), then drag and drop the necessary sections.

EDITING

I said it earlier in the book, and I'll say it again now. Editing may be the most valuable feature of the app.

Vellum offers the ability to quickly and efficiently edit a book, and it is an invaluable feature. I can't tell you how many times I've had to change something in a book after it had been converted to an eBook.

If you use someone else for formatting, it's not only time-consuming, it's expensive. You can't expect them to continually fix or add things and not charge you. But if you're doing it yourself, all it takes is a few minutes of your time.

Whether you forgot a name in the acknowledgments, spelled it wrong, forgot some other front or back matter, or a reader pointed out an error or inconsistency, Vellum makes it easy to change. And you don't need to know any code.

One time, I had a reader write to me and tell me that the subway station that I had my antagonist *go down* into, was, in fact, an above-ground stop—one of the few. I had to pay handsomely to have that changed—and I had to wait two weeks. With Vellum, I could have done it myself in one night and with zero expense.

Admittedly, if you go direct with a lot of companies the books you've fixed will involve time to re-upload to each site, but you would have to do that regardless of who fixed the error. So the question is, do you want to pay for the edit and wait a week or two? Or do you want the ability to do the edit for nothing and get it done immediately? I don't know about you, but, to me, the answer is simple—give me Vellum.

Say good-bye to mistakes forever—at least costly mistakes. You'll still have mistakes, trust me, but you'll be able to fix them yourself and eliminate that feeling of being reliant on someone else.

Other Uses

I know I titled this chapter "editing" but there are other uses that somewhat resemble editing or involve editing, which I felt should be included here.

One of those is making checklists.

What?

Yes—checklists.

Instafreebie has been the best, most magnificent service for building my mailing list. But I was frustrated that I was giving away so many books and getting so few reviewers in return. Then I thought of a different way to accomplish the same thing. I made a bunch of checklists that would have value to people within their area of expertise. I offered the checklists free—but people had to sign up to the mailing list to get them.

What kind of checklists?

Everything. But usually it had something to do with one of my books, so not only was I getting a new subscriber but I was advertising my books. Here's an abbreviated list: (By the way, the list was created with Vellum, which of course, made it easy.)

- *No Mistakes Resumes*

- *No Mistakes Interviews*
- *No Mistakes Publishing*
- *No Mistakes Formatting*
- *No Mistakes Writing*
- *Writing Shortcuts*

More checklists are coming, but for now, that's a lot to give away. I link to my books or my websites in the checklists (or both). So the *No Mistakes Resumes* checklist links to the book dealing with résumés, and the other checklists link to their appropriate books. So, yes, there will be a No Mistakes Formatting checklist which will link to this book.

The real benefit associated with Vellum is that Instafreebie only accepts ePubs. So what I do is convert the checklists to an ePub using Vellum, then upload the generated file to Instafreebie. It works perfectly. Below is a screenshot of a checklist on uploading print books. I converted it to ePub in less then ten minutes total.

part of a checklist I did

But this is not a book to sell Instafreebie. I'll do that in a future blog on my website. So hop on over to check it out, and while you're there, join the mailing list. And below, or the next page, is what the cover of the checklists looks like.

Résumé checklist

Beta Readers

Beta readers are the front line of the editing process. After you go over the book yourself, the next step should be to send your book to a small army of beta readers. If that isn't part of your process, it should be. Nothing can help improve your book better than ten or twelve strangers who will tell you the truth about what they think.

Keep in mind, these aren't people who look for typos or spelling errors. These people keep their eyes open for plot holes and inconsistencies, weak character development, factual errors, pacing, conflict, and all the other things that a content editor might look for. The difference is they won't charge you a fortune for doing it, and, they constitute a much larger portion of the reading public. A content editor is one person. Beta readers are as big a group as you can get.

So once you find a good group of beta readers, which is difficult, to say the least, how do you get your manuscript to them?

In the old days, you sent a Word file or a PDF through email and the readers would usually have to convert it or read it on the computer. With Vellum, it's much easier. Create an ePub, upload it to a site like Instafreebie, get the link, then simply give the link to interested parties. They can select to download it as a Kindle, ePub, etc. You could also opt to simply email the file.

One Final Mention

One last thing to note about editing and Vellum. I do all of my writing using Scrivener, and I used to do all of my editing that way also. When I received a file back from my editor, I would import it into Scrivener, then go through a lengthy process of comparing files, etc. Then, I would export it as a .docx when I was done.

Now, all I do is take the editor's file, import it into a file in Vellum that I made for editing (similar to the aforementioned "back-matter file"), and put it side-by-side with the file that needs editing. Then I simply transfer the edits over and I never have to switch screens. (You could also do the edits in Word and then transfer it, but I despise working in Word.)

The screenshot below (or on the next page) will show what it looks like.

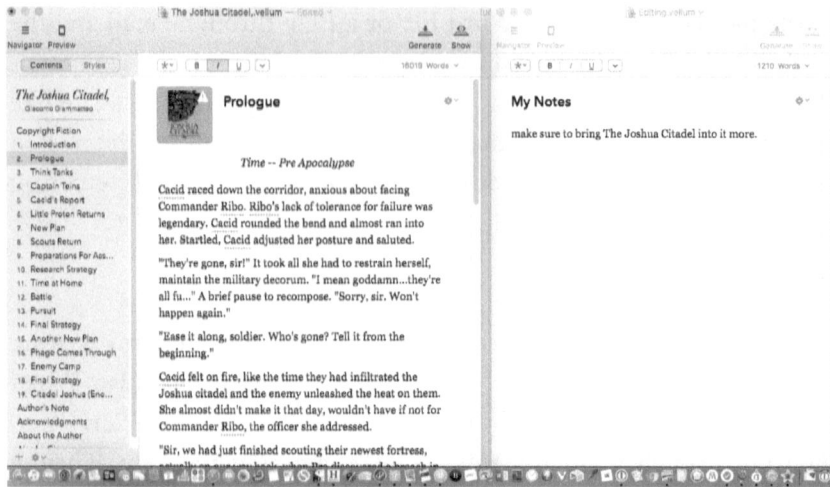

The right side of the screen shows a Vellum file that simply gives me a note to remind me what to focus on while editing. That file is where I put all of my beta reader comments though.

The screenshot below this shows the navigator pane for the file I created for editing and feedback. If I click on *Murder Is Invisible*, for example, I can access all the feedback that beta readers for that book gave me. From there, I can easily make changes to the main Vellum file, then regenerate files to produce updated eBooks in whatever format I choose.

▼ Editing
   1. My Notes
▼ Beta reader comments, all...
   ▼ How to Publish an eBook
     1. Jay Artale
     1. Murder Is Invisible...
   ▼ Memories For Sale
     2. Jeanne's comme...
The Joshua Citadel

I often do this with both eBook files and with checklist files that I use for giving away.

One thing to note. I've only experienced this with checklists, but when trying to import them, the files get messed up and separate into dozens of supposed chapters. I assume this is due to the fact that I use a lot of ✓s or ✗s or other forms of indicating lists. Perhaps Vellum sees them as chapter breaks? Anyway, the results look like the screenshot below.

screenshot of faulty import

In any case, it's an easy fix. Simply create a blank chapter and copy and paste the information you want. You wouldn't want to do this for an entire book, so if you ever experience this issue for more than a chapter or two, I would suggest reading the online help or writing to Vellum's magnificent customer support. I'm sure you'll receive a quick and satisfactory response.

GENERATE EBOOKS

Now that you're almost done, how do you get your books out of Vellum. I'm happy to report that it couldn't be easier. And I mean that. I can't think of *anything* to make this process easier.

Once you're done editing, adding back and front matter, images, etc., then simply navigate to the File menu and select Generate eBooks or, go to the top right of the Preview pane and hit the Generate button. Either one will produce the results you want.

You'll be presented with a dialogue box that looks like this:

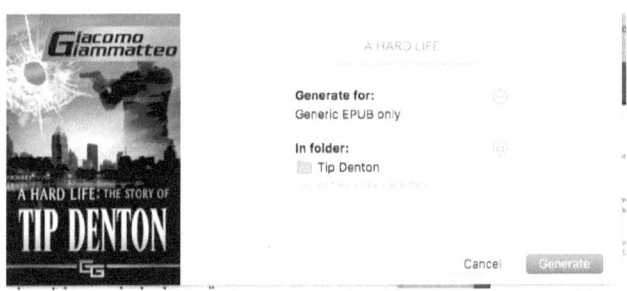

Generate menu, with cover image included

As you can see, it includes your cover image on the left, and it asks which type of books you want to generate. The above screenshot shows Generic only because I was going to use an aggregator (Smashwords) to distribute the book to Apple, Nook, Kobo, and others. If I had been going direct, I would click the button next to that, which presents you with the option shown below, allowing you to choose any of the five at the top.

Select platforms for generation:

- iBooks
- Nook
- Kindle
- Google Play
- Kobo
- ✓ Generic EPUB
  Use for aggregators and other stores

Options for Generate menu

Once you make a selection of what kind of files (books) you want, then you're given the option of *where* to export them. In which folder?

In this case, I have created a folder called Tip Denton in my Fiction/Mysteries section where it will be easy for me to find.

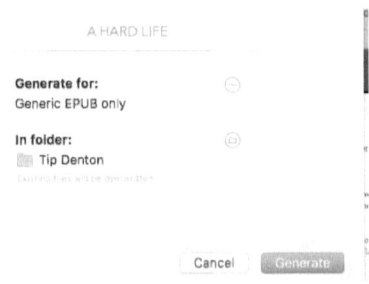

More generate menu screenshots

HOW TO FORMAT AN EBOOK

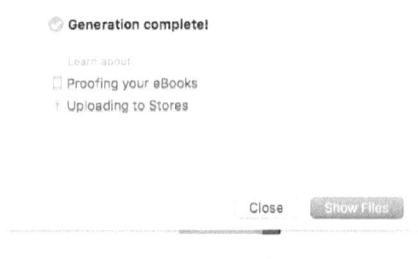

More generate menu screenshots

You are now presented with a dialogue that lets you know the generation of the files is complete and offers links to information about proofing your books and uploading to stores.

At this time, you can also use the menu or the button on the top right-hand side of the Preview pane and select Show Files which will take you immediately to the generated files.

It's worth noting here that the last time I used Vellum to generate books for specific stores, it only took seven seconds. That's *seven* seconds to produce five gorgeous eBooks. I was impressed.

Not Just For Retail

Let's take a moment here to mention something. There are many reasons why a person might want a Kindle version of an eBook or an ePub. I've listed a few below:

- ARCs (Advanced Reading Copies)
- Mailing List builders (to use as giveaways to build the list)
- Beta readers (fantastic use)
- Proofreaders
- Editors (If you have one that will edit on an iPad)

Being able to use an eBook for the above purposes is a huge advantage. Let's face it, in this day and age, almost everyone has either a Kindle or something they can read an ePub on. This feature provides an easy way to quickly get your files to your people.

And if you combine it with services like Instafreebie or Bookfunnel to help build a mailing list, it can be invaluable.

Book Tours

If you decide to partake in a virtual book tour, Vellum is great. It will allow you to provide the necessary files, no matter what kind, then use a site like Instafreebie to distribute them or simply email the books.

Editors and Proofreaders

If you have editors and proofreaders that agree to do their work on an iPad or any tablet that is compatible with yours (if you have one) then it can save you a lot of time. I have a proofreader who uses it, and she swears it saves her time. It certainly helps me.

Most editors seem to have an aversion to new things, though, and prefer to use Word.

IN CLOSING

Needless to say, I'm a huge fan of Vellum. It has saved me a tremendous amount of time and trouble.

I won't say that every one of you will experience the same results, but you should be able to quickly get up-to-speed, and there is no reason why you can't produce your first eBook within twenty-four hours.

Although Vellum's help menu is a wonderful resource, I hope you've learned few things you might not have learned otherwise. And although this book doesn't cover things that may pop up during the normal course of working with Vellum, things like import problems and how to fix those problems, rest assured there are easy ways to fix almost anything that crops up, and accessing Vellum's help page or writing to customer service will do the trick. Below is a screenshot of what the main help page looks like, and here is the link:

Getting Started

Vellum Tutorial
Importing Your Manuscript

Editing & Formatting

Chapter Headings
Adding Text Features
    Inline Images
    Store Links
Creating Box Sets

Title and Author Information
Cover Image Requirements
Your Table of Contents

Generating & Uploading

Generating eBooks
Proofing Your eBooks
Troubleshooting eBooks

Uploading to Stores
Advance Reader Copies

screenshot from Vellum's website

Also, if you want to proof your final product, you can, of course, use Apple's desktop reading app, or you can use an iPad, iPhone, or the Kindle Reading app. If you need to proof for a Nook or Kobo app, Vellum has excellent suggestions on how to do that on their website. You can go here.

The bottom line?

Vellum will...

- Save you money
- Save you time
- Decrease frustration

You can't ask for much more than that.

In case I haven't mentioned it, Vellum has some of the best customer support I've ever used. I took full advantage of it when writing this book and they were magnificent.

Vellum has changed my books forever. I am now using images extensively to add flavor to all my books.

Below is an image showing a series of four screenshots, two of them are inline images that I used in my mystery books to depict the places I was talking about, and the other two are chapter headings, delineating POV—the gun for third person and the bullet for first person.

I haven't launched any books like this yet, but I have several on preorder. The beta readers who read the books loved them. I'm hoping others do as well.

i nodded. "That's the key. He's not gonna kill
body who spends millions of dollars at his
o. You don't kill the goose that lays the
m eggs."

unless the goose is reaching sterility," Lou said.

it the hell does that mean?"

n't know," Lou said. "But we'll find out. I'll have
sic accounting go through all of their books
a fine-toothed comb. They'll find something.
usually do."

INVESTIGATION SHOWED that WOW sold expen-
paintings to each of the dead men. Manual
rez bought one for about 1.4 million. It was a
re of a vineyard set in the rolling hills of
iny with a newly restored villa as the backdrop.

Monfrer bought one for 800,000, a beautiful la
scape of Lake Champlain when the leaves w
turning color, and Farmington purchased a sti
ning picture of the Brooklyn Bridge while it v
under construction, and during a fierce snowstor
That set him back more than 1.1 million.

By the way, the book you just read was formatted using Vellum. And it was done in one evening. If you're interested in buying Vellum—and you should be—click on this link.

A t this time, as previously noted, Vellum does not have an app to create a PDF for either IngramSpark or CreateSpace, but one is forthcoming, and I'm sure it will be just as good as this one is; in fact, I've been beta testing it, and it is as good as this. It's fantastic.

They also do not have an app for PCs; Vellum is MAC only. But you could *run a simulation program, or borrow a MAC (or steal one if you have to.), but no matter what you have to do, it will be worth it.*

If all else fails, and you can't get your hands on a MAC to use, check out my website. I do formatting and it's guaranteed as long as you provide a decent file to begin with. If you don't like it, you don't pay. Simple as that.

ACKNOWLEDGMENTS

It is with great honor that I give eternal gratitude to my wife Mikki and all four of my grandkids: Giuseppe, Dante, Adalina, and Carmine. They give me the inspiration to keep going.

Also to the following people for the great input I received: Jay Artale, David Penny, and Jeanne Haskin. You helped make the book better.

ALSO BY GIACOMO GIAMMATTEO

You can see all of my books here.
And you can buy them on the platform of your choice here.

Nonfiction:

No Mistakes Resumes, Book I of *No Mistakes Careers*

No Mistakes Interviews, Book II of *No Mistakes Careers*

Misused Words, No Mistakes Grammar, Volume I

Misused Words for Business, No Mistakes Grammar, Volume II

More Misused Words, No Mistakes Grammar, Volume III

No Mistakes Writing, Volume I—Writing Shortcuts

How to Publish an eBook, No Mistakes Publishing, Volume I

How to Format an eBook, No Mistakes Publishing, Volume II

eBook Distribution, No Mistakes Publishing, Volume III

Uneducated

Fiction:

Friendship & Honor Series:

Murder Takes Time

Murder Has Consequences

Murder Takes Patience

Murder Is Invisible

Blood Flows South Series:

A Bullet For Carlos: A Connie Gianelli Mystery

Finding Family, a Novella

A Bullet From Dominic

Redemption Series:

Necessary Decisions: A Gino Cataldi Mystery

Old Wounds

Promises Kept, the Story of Number Two

Premeditated

OTHER BOOKS COMING SOON:

You can always see the current and coming-soon books on my website.

Fiction:

A Promise of Vengeance (Fantasy)

My first fantasy, and the first book in a four-book series—the Rules of Vengeance. (Three are already written and the fourth is being outlined.)

Titles for the fantasy series are as follows:

Undeniable Vengeance

Consummate Vengeance

Vengeance is Mine

A Hard Life, the Story of Tip Denton

Memories for Sale (mystery/sf)

The Joshua Citadel (SF novella)

Nonfiction:

Whiskers and Bear—Volume I of the Life on the Farm Series (sent to editor)

No Mistakes Writing, How to Write a Bestseller

Children's Books:

No Mistakes Grammar for Kids, Volume I—Much and Many (Sent to editor)

No Mistakes Grammar for Kids, Volume II—Lie and Lay (Sent to editor)

No Mistakes Grammar for Kids, Volume III—Then and Than (Sent to editor)

Shinobi Goes to School—Life on the Farm for Kids. (working on illustrations)

Fiona Gets Caught—Life on the Farm for Kids (being edited)

Coco Gets a Doughnut—Life on the Farm for Kids (being edited)

Biscotti Saves Punch—Life on the Farm for Kids (being edited)

Get on the mailing list and you'll be sure to be notified of release dates and sales.

Mailing list

And don't forget to leave a review!

ABOUT THE AUTHOR

Giacomo Giammatteo is the author of gritty crime dramas about murder, mystery, and family. He also writes nonfiction books including the No Mistakes Careers series.

When Giacomo isn't writing, he's helping his wife take care of the animals on their sanctuary. At last count they had 40 animals—7 dogs, a horse, 6 cats, and 25 pigs.

Oh, and one crazy—and very large—wild boar, who takes walks with Giacomo every day and happens to also be his best buddy.

nomistakespublishing.com
gg@giacomog.com

www.ingramcontent.com/pod-product-compliance
Lightning Source LLC
Chambersburg PA
CBHW021156080526
44588CB00008B/369